For Such a Time as This

The Message of Esther

Evelyn Booth-Clibborn

New Wine Press

©1990 Evelyn Booth-Clibborn

New Wine Press
P.O. Box 17
Chichester PO20 6YB
England

Unless otherwise stated Scripture Quotations are
from the Revised Standard Version, Copyright©
Churches of Christ in the United States of
America.

Scripture Quotations marked AV are from the
Authorised Version.

British Library Cataloguing in Publication Data
Booth-Clibborn, Evelyn
　For such a time as this.
　1. Bible. O.T. Esther. Critical studies
　I. Title
　222.906

　ISBN 0 947852 80 8

Typeset by The Ikthos Studios, Andover, Hampshire.

Printed in England by Clays Ltd, St Ives plc

Dedication

For my beloved sister, José

Contents

Page

Foreword

Just after midnight, on the Lord's Day, August 19th 1990, in her 93rd year, Evelyn Beatrice Booth-Clibborn was called into the presence of her Lord and Saviour.

We have witnessed a departure, but God has witnessed an arrival. My task is to honour this rare and gracious Christian lady.

I believe, first, that even if her grandfather had not been General William Booth and her mother the devoted Maréchale we should still thank God for every remembrance of her. God's word requires that *"the righteous shall be (held) in everlasting remembrance"* (Psalm 112:6 AV).

But secondly, I believe also that Evelyn would shoot me at the dawn of glory if I did not above all, in this tribute, preach her Christ, her Jesus, her Lord and Saviour. For the motto of her life was clearly *"for me to live is Christ, to die is to gain"* (Philippians 1:21).

She once said that she was the black sheep of the family. In 1922 she headed across the Atlantic to America to embark upon a musical career as a concert pianist. By the early Thirties she made her début in New York, where she received favourable reviews.

But not from God. At that time she was far from God, by her own admission. Her mother requested her several times to accompany her on some of the evangelistic campaigns that she was engaged in. But her career came first.

Then came that amazing crisis and crossroads in Evelyn's life. The verses of scripture that spoke to her were Isaiah 43:18,19, *"Remember ye not the former things, neither consider the things of old. Behold I will do a new thing; now it shall spring forth; shall ye not know it? I will make a way in the wilderness, and rivers in the desert"* This was a dramatic turning point.

Just before the beginning of the Second World War she returned to this country. She lived with her mother at the Haven in Devon, and was with her right up to her last moment. In the late fifties she came to Slavanka Christian Guest House in Bournemouth, where in a sense she launched out into the deep. She began those piano recitals and talks, which for over twenty years brought so much blessing to so many people.

In 1987 she moved from Slavanka to Seacliff Court. Friends had the honour and the joy of being there with her when she celebrated her 90th birthday. But she saw it differently. She realised that it was the jubilee of her dedicated life to her Saviour, "50 years for Jesus", which is the title and striking note of her recent autobiography.

She was a great person for witnessing on

trains. She had an expression, "the Lord does know how to break the ice". Before reaching her destination she would most likely have handed a John's Gospel to someone; and more than once a silence has fallen upon the whole carriage as her bell-like voice rang out clearly in proclaiming some truth about her Saviour.

She played on all kinds of pianos, from broken-down ones in draughty halls to finely-tuned grand pianos in drawing rooms. She never murmured, but turned missing notes into something worthy for the Lord.

Her connection with the Girl Crusaders' Union was a long-standing and fruitful one. How many women, now bringing up families of their own, and in different professions, can thank God that she ministered Christ to them in their youth? Some would remember those amazing Sunday nights at Aberlour Camp in Scotland, when she would play the piano, and lead camper and officer alike into the presence of God, in praise of her Saviour.

She was very much a team person, working happily with others, whether at camps or conferences, or on her many recital-talk tours. Miss Isobel Macdonald, a former General Secretary of the Girl Crusaders' Union, summed up 50 years of fellowship and service together with her in these words, "We thank God for a life lived for Him, and laid down for others." We need more people like that.

No-one could be so used of God without paying a tremendous price. She was a most talented person; one of God's artists. What it must have cost her to live constantly in the public eye, particularly as she had no home-life. She was always the messenger in the message, literally. She knew God, she proved God, and the constant message of her life was victory with God. Evelyn's life-verse was, *"But thanks be to God, who gives us the victory through our Lord Jesus Christ"* (1 Corinthians 15:57).

She was a lady of exceptional spiritual perception, yet so caring. For her, personal work was *personal* work – in this sense – sympathy seems too thin a word; there was empathy. She entered into the deeper feelings of whoever needed her help. She never made much of herself. She had that rare ability to draw others out, and encourage them by her own inspiration and blessing. Her great love for people was evidenced in her bracing and faithful criticism when necessary. She never dodged an issue.

There was an amazing balance in her life. When you looked upon her, heard her speak, met her privately, you had the impression of such strength. Yet it was a disciplined tenderness, so loving and caring; and the discipline and love were not in tension, let alone in conflict. *"Thy gentleness has made me great"* (Psalm 18:35) would be her testimony.

We all have our memories of unforgettable incidents and quotes. Nearing the end of a talk she gave on David and Goliath, she dramatised, *"Who is this uncircumcised Philistine that he should defy the armies of the living God?"*

(1 Samuel 17:26). And reaching the climax, she pronounced, "David looked upon Goliath and reduced him to a question mark!"

The last occasion I saw Evelyn was in May. It took my friend and I over an hour to locate Seacliff Court, which reduced our time with her. But we shall never forget that visit. Her unforgettable words were, "I'm on top with Jesus, and there's nowhere else to be!"

Her last words to a close friend were, "Remember, by the cross, by the blood, by the blessed Spirit, we are going on!"

She lived in constant sight of the cross, in awed wonder; and the cross of Christ and His blood were the constant theme of her life.

"She lay in dust life's glory dead
And from the cross there blossomed red
Life that shall endless be."
George Matheson

For Evelyn Booth-Clibborn there are three certainties. First, her death was a victory and not a defeat. In fact she never saw death, because she proved the amazing words of her Saviour in John 8:51, *"Verily, verily, I say unto you, 'If a man keep my saying, he shall never see death'"* (AV).

There is a nuance there which means this. Evelyn did not focus on death, but on the conqueror of death, the victor of death, even the Lord Jesus Christ. She never tasted death, because Christ has not only taken the sting out of death, which is sin, but He has taken the taste out of it. Death is tasteless to a believer.

In verse 52 of that same chapter it reads, "*If a man keep my saying, he shall never taste of death.*" Christ has tasted death for everyone who trusts in Him.

Secondly, her death was a gain and not a loss. "*Christ shall be magnified in my body, whether it be by life, or by death. For me to live is Christ, and to die is gain.*" So reads Philippians 1:20, 21 (AV), and it goes on to say, "*having a desire to depart, and to be with Christ; which is far better.*"

Thirdly, her death was a glorious beginning and not a terrible, fearful ending. Jesus said in those wonderfully comforting words of John 11:25,26, "*I am the resurrection, and the life: he that believeth in me, though he were dead, yet shall he live: and whosoever liveth and believeth in me shall never die. Believest thou this?*" (AV).

Evelyn knew that the manuscript of "Esther", which she had given as Bible studies and talks over the years, was to be published in book form. From the first moment the manuscript was taken out of the drawer, she expressed an innocent joy in hearing it read to her again. "Did I really write that?" she would say with unfamiliar pride.

Those who cared so lovingly for Evelyn, during her last days at Seacliff Court, were able to tell her that the book was complete, just before she was too ill to take it in.

Even while in hospital, knowing of the

progress of the book, she said something which I believe was her dying conviction, "At least, I will have done something in making 'Esther' known."

That greater conviction surely is this, *"I have glorified Thee upon the earth. I have finished the work Thou gavest Me to do"* (John 17:4 AV).

It is wonderful that men and women are immortal until their work is done.

How refreshing to read a ninety-two year old woman with a message for today's increasingly pagan society. Yet those of us who have had the privilege of knowing E.B-C (as she is affectionately known) are not surprised. For many years she has held audiences of all ages spellbound by her moving piano recitals and talks, which have spoken directly to the hearts and lives of her hearers. Either she never heard of the 'generation gap' or else she crossed it with her eyes closed. Her perpetual dwelling place has been 'on top' with Jesus. Evelyn Booth-Clibborn's "Esther" steps out into our world. We meet her face to face on every page, and she leads us by the hand back into her world. In a very readable and relevant way, she shows us that we don't have to capitulate to the trends of modern society or wish we had been born in another day of history. Rather, her "Esther" calls us back from this age, which doesn't want to get too involved in anything, to a new and total commitment to Christ. She makes us realise that we have been born "for *such a time as this*" (Esther 4:14), and that we must live for God before it is too late.

Rev. Paul T.A. Bassett, B.D.,
Melbourne Hall Evangelical Free Church,
St. Peter's Road / Melbourne Road,
Leicester.
August, 1990.

Chapter 1

Setting the Scene

(Esther Chapter 1:1-22)

The book of "Esther" is a success story, set against a background of extreme wealth and magnificence. To God circumstances have little importance; to man, they matter very much indeed. When tempted to envy those better off than ourselves, we might well remember that wealth and position can be a hindrance to spirituality. *"How hard it is for those who have riches to enter into the kingdom of God"* (Luke 18:24), said Jesus to His disciples on looking upon the rich young ruler.

The first chapter sets the scene. It is one of unimaginable luxury and lavishness. The king, in order to impress his distinguished visitors, *"showed them the riches of his royal glory and the splendour and pomp of his majesty"* for no less than a hundred and eighty days, and after that came the banquet for *"both great and small"* in the palace gardens, lasting seven successive days. Some description of the furnishings is given, but even so it is impossible for us to envisage this oriental magnificence. Time was of no consequence; display was what mattered, and the leisurely enjoyment of sensual pleasures. At the heart of it all were the king's pride and the king's prestige.

Nor was this all. The queen, who was beautiful and a very important part of that royal prestige, was now to be shown off to peoples and princes; hence the king's command that she should appear before them. But the queen refused to obey that command. Surely something unheard of. We do not know her reason, which may well have been a deep reluctance to being exhibited in this way before a great crowd of men, even though they were the king's guests. Whatever the reason, in the king's sight, the action was unpardonable, a terrible insult to his person. He was furious and *"his anger burned within him"*.

Ahasuerus was a pagan, and not in the remotest sense a godly man. Yet how often, as Christians with all the light that this implies, are we upset if things go against the accepted pattern. It can indeed be difficult not to be affected if something wrong or seemingly out of place has occurred. What we may fail to realise, in the heat of the moment, is that God may well have a purpose in allowing that trying experience. Queen Vashti had to go to make room for Esther. The old order had to give way to the new. This can be a painful experience, whether for Queen Vashti or for us.

Every experience in the Christian life has a lesson. How much better if that lesson is well and truly learned. Wonderful things were to happen: good was to triumph, justice was to be done, a whole nation was to be saved from destruction.

The last phase of Vashti's career as queen was a sad one. Her action in refusing to obey the king was probably based on fine womanly sensibilities. After all, she was the king's wife, in a very high and honoured position, to which he alone could have raised her. Nevertheless her refusal to obey him was, for her, a very grave mistake. Her whole position was from that moment entirely and irrevocably changed.

Though there is no doubt that the king's pride far outreached his love for his wife, which can happen only too easily in the closest human relationships, there was also the question of example. It was not to be tolerated in those days that a wife should stand up to the unquestioned authority of one who considered himself her lord and master. This breach of the accepted code of conduct must be shown up at once and in the most forceful terms. He turned to the seven wisest and most honoured men in his kingdom. Queen Vashti must go; and it must be written that she must go, written "among the law of the Persians and Medes, so that it may not be altered". This was the final stamp upon her dismissal.

From a position of dazzling height, commanding continual attention and adulation, she is suddenly plunged into the deepest obscurity to be unheeded and unnoticed. From a world of all possibly luxuries, every whim catered for, every desire studied and met, she is reduced to a life whose very deprivations would be, by contrast, a continual reminder of what she had lost. She would suffer an abiding humiliation.

In this first verse of chapter two, we are told that the king remembered Vashti (just "Vashti" now) and what she had done and what had been decreed against her. Did he also remember to look after and protect her in her loneliness? This may have been the case, but we are not told that he did. On the contrary the king's eyes were already looking ahead. Vashti's place must be filled, and quickly.

There are some hard facts in life. One of them is the frequent fickleness of human nature. Sudden and surprising changes occur, with overtones of cruelty and callousness which are hard to explain. Selfish considerations, based on a deep-seated pride, of which a person may not even be aware, can lie at the heart of them.

Since Ahasuerus was a pagan king, it would be quite unrealistic to expect too much of him. Sadly, human nature over the intervening centuries has remained the same. Even as Christians, have we not known such experiences: the callous word which was meant to hurt; the brusque manner checking the kind approach; the proud, unforgiving spirit cleaving the relationship? Let there be no mistake, they are all chips off the same block that supplied the cross.

No wonder the apostle Paul, beholding that hard substance which is the ego, the self, cried: *"Who shall deliver me?"* (Romans 7:24). This is our cry, too, when we view our hearts with their pride, their smugness and their deceptions.

But the apostle had a shining answer to his question. It was *"Thanks be to God through our Lord Jesus Christ"*. He writes to the Philippians, *"For His sake I have suffered the loss of all things* (including self-pleasing), *and count them as refuse, that I may gain Christ and be found in Him"* (Philippians 3:8,9). That is the secret of victory: *"Not I, but Christ"* (Galatians 2:20).

Chapter 2

You Can Afford to Wait

(Esther Chapter 2: 1-20)

Queen Vashti has gone. Who is to take her place? The king's personal servants make a suggestion: let fair young maidens be sought out for the king, and let those he appoints as officers gather them to the harem in Susa, the capital; let the maiden who pleases the king most be queen instead of Vashti. This is agreeable to the king, and he does as they suggest.

At this point, another person is introduced into the story, one who is to play a vital part, Mordecai. Even as Nehemiah could never have rebuilt the walls of Jerusalem without his brethren, so Esther could never have delivered the Jewish people without Mordecai. In this case, one man was to be more effective than a hundred brethren. Numbers matter little to God. It is the willingness of His chosen servants to work as members of the one body, and as His fellow-workers.

Mordecai was a Jew, a Benjamite, who along with other captives had been carried away from Jerusalem by Nebuchadnezzar. When Esther's father and mother died, Mordecai adopted her and brought her up as his own daughter. At the outset this tells us a good deal about Mordecai. He was unselfish, tender-hearted and willing to take on the responsibility of bringing up a girl, not easy for a man on his own. But if, as we surmise, he was a good man, he was also a wise one.

Esther, being beautiful, had been chosen with the other maidens to be brought to the Palace. Because Mordecai had instructed her not to do so, she did not divulge her Jewish nationality to anyone. This instruction reveals the perceptive-ness of Mordecai. First, he was aware of the precarious position of Jews; secondly, he did not want anything to prevent Esther from reaching a position of power; thirdly, he saw that, if ever she did become queen, this might have far-reaching repercussions for the Jewish people.

Moreover, Mordecai was a patient man. He was patient because he had a long-term view. He could afford to wait. It did not mean that immediate matters were not attended to, but they were seen in perspective, and did not assume too much importance. There was a calmness, a steadfastness, about his anticipation of the future.

It is good for the Christian to have a goal, and what higher goal than the glory of God and the extension of His kingdom? To have such an over-all objective enables us to be patient, to take the snubs, the disappointments, the frustrations, knowing that as we overcome, by His grace, each victory, however small, glorifies Him and extends His kingdom.

But there was another reason why Mordecai could wait. He was also a humble man. Although he was Esther's father, in every respect but birth, wiser and more experienced, neither is his seniority stressed, nor are his opinions aired. He did not stand in the way of God's purposes. Quietly, every day, while Esther was gaining favour and position, he would walk in front of the court of the harem and ask how Queen Esther was getting on. He must have done this with much tact and courtesy; yet must also have endured many a snub. Nothing deterred him. The daily, monotonous action continued. It was a hidden ministry.

"You have been faithful over a little, I will set you over much." (Matthew 25:23). There is no finer training both in humility and in patience than to be faithful over a few things, in small matters to be unnoticed, unpraised. Jesus said, *"I am among you as one who serves"* (Luke 22:27). So humble did He consider this ministry of service to be, that He did not refer to Himself by name, but merely as *"one who serves"*.

Esther was put under Hegai, who was in charge of the women, and it is here we are given our first glimpse into her character. We read that Esther *"pleased Hegai and won his favour"*. Now Hegai had

23

many fair maidens in his care, but we are not told that all of them won his approval. Therefore, it could not have been merely Esther's outward appearance which counted. Such was his favour that Esther was promoted to the best place in the harem, and provided with whatever she needed. She was to achieve great heights in the promotion to come, but first had to win approval on the humblest level.

This reminds us of Joseph who found favour with Potiphar, one of Pharaoh's officers. He made him over-seer of his entire household (Genesis 39:4). This was well before Joseph came into power. There are no short cuts in God's programme.

That Esther won Hegai's approval in the daily life of the harem implied that she was of a docile disposition, easy to teach, willing to obey. How often does a lack of pliability hold us back in the Christian life, so that lessons which were never learnt have to be repeated over and over again.

Esther was also discreet. There must have been a good deal of chatter when the maidens were alone, with plenty of questions thrown in. After all, they were young and the situation was unusual. But Esther, even if tempted to talk, never gave away her secret. No one knew that she was Jewish, probably the only Jew among them all. What a wonderful asset discretion is to any woman or man. When used, how many thousands of hurtful or mischievous words would be left unspoken, misunderstandings and tragedies avoided.

"Now Esther found favour in the eyes of all who saw her". This was one of the most positive and revealing statements made concerning Esther. "All" must have included the maidens who were not as successful in winning Hegai's favour. This implied an endearing quality about Esther that outshone her beauty, which by itself could easily have aroused envy or jealousy. This predominant characteristic triumphed over all other assets, and attracted rather than repelled.

Joseph (as we saw earlier) had this same quality; and what of Christ, our supreme example, in whom it was perfectly manifested? We read of His early years: *"And Jesus increased in wisdom and in stature, and in favour with God and man"* (Luke 2:52). In each case, that of Esther, Joseph and Christ Himself, the position of power and authority was preceded by the docility, discretion and wisdom which won the favour of all with whom they lived or worked.

What a lesson and a challenge for us. *"And I,"* said Jesus, *"when I am lifted up from the earth, will draw all men to myself."* (John 12:32). Even though this referred primarily to the cross, there is a sense in which Christ, indwelling the Christian, can be so "lifted up" as to draw men and women to Himself. If such is His purpose, what room should there be within us for that which contrariwise offends and repels? There is most certainly the *"offence of the cross"*, but we are not told that we ourselves should offend or repel. On the contrary, our Lord told us it is the peacemakers who are blessed; and Paul's injunction to the Galatians was, *"through love be servants of one another"* (Galatians 5:13).

The preparation of Esther was nearing its end. *"The king"*, we read, *" loved Esther more than all the women. . . so that he set the royal crown on her head and made her queen instead of Vashti"*. Her triumph was complete. She now occupied the throne Vashti had lost; Esther's position was next only to that of the king. She could command every luxury, attention or delicacy she desired. As if to underline her new status, the king gave a great banquet specially in her honour; it was to be known as "Esther's Banquet". The people were to share in the rejoicing, as the king granted them remission of taxes and liberally bestowed gifts upon them.

Note the effect of all this in Esther. Did an exaggerated pride enter her soul or a certain aloofness enter her attitude towards Mordecai, that humble man walking down there outside the palace court? If so, there was no sign of it. Rather, we are told that she kept her nationality secret, *"as Mordecai had charged her"*. These very significant words are added: *"for Esther obeyed Mordecai just as when she was brought up by him"*. Here indeed lay the secret of that which was docile, discreet and attractive in her character, which won the favour of all who met her. Neither the deference towards Mordecai's superior wisdom nor the obedience she had always given him had changed.

This is unusual. Esther was a full-grown woman and had reached a very high position. Has not every mature person a right to his or her independence? On the human level everyone has a right. But there is a higher level that is sometimes forgotten. The truth is that Esther's life had sprung and developed from a very deep root, that of obedience to a good and wise man. It was, in fact bound up with the plan of God; and no one who is bound up with the plan of God is independent. It is quite impossible. Esther was not independent; even Jesus, on an infinitely higher level, was not independent, *"I always do what is pleasing to Him"* (John 8:29). (Note the words *"always"* and *"Him"*). This is the basic difference between living for self and living for God; between a barren and a fruitful Christian experience. It means that Paul's statement: *"Ye are not your own"* (1 Corinthians 6:19), instead of being a truth to which we give only mental assent, is an actual, living and continuing experience.

Independence, being rooted in self and not in obedience to God, sets the course of our lives in a opposite direction to that which God has planned. It drove David into terrible sin, and sent Jonah fleeing towards certain disaster.

Mordecai was God's representative to Esther. No change of circumstances, no promotion to an exalted position, no material advantages of any kind whatsoever, would be allowed to come between them or to cleave their relationship.

Would that we, too, were as faithful to God-given directives, whether imparted through men or women of God, through words of the Bible, or through outward signs in our circumstances.

Chapter 3

The Watching God

(Esther Chapter 2:21 - Chapter 3:15)

Soon after Esther became Queen an incident occurred which, in view of later developments, was of great significance. Mordecai was sitting at the king's gate when he was informed of a recent ugly event. Two of the king's eunuchs who guarded the threshold, Bigthan and Teresh, sought to lay hands on the king, because they were angry. Mordecai conveyed the news to the queen, who in turn informed the king. Having verified the facts, the king condemned both men to be hanged.

There is more to this incident than Mordecai's alertness in reporting the matter. One small phrase catches our special attention. Esther gave the king the message *"in the name of Mordecai"*. During events immediately following, that name was to be treated with the utmost contempt. But to Esther it was exceedingly precious. She apparently seized the very first opportunity of mentioning it to the king, who at once recorded it in the Book of Chronicles. This was the first tiny step towards Mordecai's eventual promotion.

We have a Name infinitely more precious. Do we seize the opportunity of mentioning it to someone who may have no personal knowledge of that Name? The king did not know of Mordecai before Esther mentioned him; at least we have no record that he did. With the Christian, the matter goes even further than that of witness. Paul says, *"Whatever you do, in word or deed, do all in the name of the Lord Jesus"* (Colossians 3:17). What a help this is with those endless decisions and their inevitable results. If our desires behind those decisions are in accordance with that Name and its honour, then the deeds that follow will glorify God. No wonder Paul adds, *"Giving thanks to God the Father through Him."* The thanks will be a daily experience. There will be so much for which to thank Him.

After the discovery of the plot against the king's life, everything looked calm enough. Haman, a highly gifted man, had already established his position with people who counted. The king would be looking for just such a man to run the affairs of state and attend to important matters. Haman's promotion to a place of power was a portent of disaster for the Jews; but God was watching over His people, and we have already caught a glimpse of how His plan was eventually to unfold.

We read, *"And all the king's servants who were at the king's gate bowed down and did obeisance to Haman"*. This was at the king's command, of course. Nevertheless, people are impressed by power and prestige; not only that, they like to go along with the crowd and comply with the 'done thing'. Mordecai did not bow down or do obeisance. A shattering offence. The king's servants were appalled. Daily they spoke to him about it, but to no avail. Why would Mordecai not bow down? Here we see something of both his godliness and his courage. Haman was an Amalekite, and in the time of Moses God had declared perpetual war on the Amalekites. It was God's command, not the king's. God was Mordecai's final authority for his conduct, whatever the cost to himself.

That is what we need so desperately, men and women who are loyal to their convictions, who believe in the supreme authority of God and are willing to obey that authority at whatever cost to themselves. We are being increasingly threatened by destructive forces. The challenge is to us personally. Our loyalty to God must come first.

The king's servants, having failed in their repeated attempts to persuade Mordecai to bow down, decided that they should tell Haman about his refusal to do so, mentioning at the same time that he was a Jew. Incidentally, is it not 'the king's servants', those little nagging, persistent words, that so often wear down our resistance?

Haman's fury when told of Mordecai's default was not to stop at this one man, but was to embrace the whole of the Jewish population, the people whom he now purposed to destroy.

Two facts have come to the fore. The first is that pride is most clearly revealed when we are suddenly challenged. This basic sin can lie hidden in the heart for years, unrecognised or subtly disguised, until what we feel to be our rights are threatened. Then, something akin to hatred, in word if not in deed, may rear its ugly head. Haman did not know God; he was just an evil man. Lucifer knew God (in part, that is) and was the highest of all the angels. Even in so glorious an abode, it was pride that hurled him from the highest realm into deepest darkness.

Secondly, if that sudden challenge revealed the strength of Haman's pride, it also showed the extent of the harm resulting from that pride, which was to affect a whole nation. Offended self-love can be like a fire in the soul burning up ourselves and others too for sheer need of fuel on which to expend itself. Haman's is an extreme case, but the basic fact remains.

Since this sin presents a danger to us all, what can be done about it? Next to prayer and reliance upon God's saving power, there are two guiding principles. The first is not to cling to even the dearest of God's gifts, whether personal or material, but to hand it over to God, consciously and regularly. The second is not to expect anything from anyone by way of recognition or reward for what may have been achieved.

Is not humility infinitely more attractive than pride? How much more effective for God is the humble Mordecai walking patiently outside the palace court than a hundred Hamans strutting about in their pride and glory!

The rage which Haman felt because of Mordecai's default in refusing to bow down to him did not prevent a cold and calculated preparation for the realisation of his evil designs. As soon as the auspicious moment for his approach to the king had been decided upon, this "enemy of the Jews" was ready to seize his opportunity for gaining the royal approval for his plan.

"There is a certain people scattered abroad and dispersed among the peoples in all the provinces of your kingdom," he now informed the king, *"their laws are different from those of every other people, and they do not keep the king's laws, so that it is not for the king's profit to tolerate them. If it please the king,"* he continued, *" let it be decreed that they be destroyed, and I will pay ten thousand talents of silver into the hands of those who have charge of the king's business, that they may put it into the king's treasuries."*

This was a very subtle speech, which won immediate royal approval. We read that the king straightaway took his signet ring from his hand and gave it to Haman, granting him, not only the money, but also the Jewish people.

In brief, the king gave him both the authority to act, with the money to forward that act, and the people on which it was to be carried out. Everything was now in Haman's power. It was a formidable triumph. Indeed, so convincing was he that the king did not even seek to verify the facts, as he had done over Mordecai's report of the threat to his royal person. After all, Ahasuerus was a pagan king. In his eyes, what would be the loss of a thousand Jewish lives compared to his own safety?

Nevertheless, the swiftness with which this commission had been granted to Haman was startling. Why should he have had this outstanding success? True, a powerful and satanic spirit possessed him, a rage that was utterly evil and very dangerous; but all this would not have availed had there not been the most careful preparation for the attaining of his objective. Jesus said, *"The children of this world in their own generation are wiser than the children of light"* (Luke 16:8 AV).

First was the careful timing. There was to be no hurry about it. Lots were cast day after day, month after month. They had to be sure of the auspicious time for Haman's approach to the king. Secondly, there was the careful wording of the speech, with just enough deviation from the truth to further Haman's ends. Thirdly, there was the subtle appeal to the king's pride, *"It is not for the king's profit to tolerate them"*. And fourthly, came the final inducement. Haman offered his own money. This may well have been what tipped the scales on the side of his plan.

As Christians, we are possessed of an entirely different spirit, and are constrained by love instead of hate; our trust is in God, and not in our own understanding. Even so, do we give the same kind of care and thoroughness in the working out of His thought and plan? How important it is that we should be sure of His timing before starting on some new project; that our words relating to that project should be His kind of words; and that the final inducement to action should come as His prompting. This may be by some statement from His word, through one of His servants, or by some strong inner urging of the Spirit.

We are told, *"God is at work in you, both to will and to work for His good pleasure"* (Philippians 2:13). This is our source of strength, our very assurance. But how important it is that we should work out what He works in. That this working out should be *"with fear and trembling"* implies a total dependence upon God, and much care and discipline in the personal life.

Having secured the royal favour for his plan, Haman approached the zenith of his power. Until now there had been no need for haste. Thoroughness and efficiency were what was most needed. From the moment he received his commission from the king, events began to move rapidly.

Foundation work does not come again, once

completed. Hence its importance.

An edict written according to Haman's command was sent in the king's name, sealed with the king's ring, to the governors of all the provinces. Its contents were that all Jews, young and old, women and children, were to be slain, destroyed, annihilated in one day, the thirteenth day of the twelfth month in the month of Adar. No time to be lost. The king and Haman sat down to drink. The decree was on its way. The coming massacre was assured; the job was as good as done. Now for a little recreation.

Are we not reminded here of a similar time of recreation? They had spat on Him, driven nails into His hands and feet, fastened Him securely to the cross, and that was that. They could sit down and just watch Him there. For them it was the end. How could they know that the salvation of the world was being wrought out on that very cross, even as they watched, and that the resurrection, the power and the glory lay just ahead? And how could the king and Haman know that, even as they were drinking in the flush of seeming triumph, a great deliverance of thousands whom they had condemned to death was about to take place?

How often, when grief, disappointment or some wrong course of action seem to bring us to a complete and devastating end, we see only that end and its apparent destruction of all hope and confidence. And all the time God is working towards a deliverance. God is far greater than any enemy, and His desire is always to save the lost. How little we know and understand our God!

Even as that massive destruction had been planned by just two people, so God would work His deliverance by just two people. He is the greatest and most efficient of all executives. We need not fear the outward danger, however deep and extensive, nor the seeming defeat or isolation of our position. What we do need to fear is that anything should lessen our complete inner dependence on God.

Perhaps God allows us to reach 'dead ends' that we might discover our own utter insufficiency. It is good that we are weak, because then we are strong. When Paul came up against the extremities of circumstances, he was able to say, *"I can do all things through Christ who strengthens me"* (Philippians 4:13).

Chapter 4

God Shows the Way Out

(Esther Chapter 4:1 - Chapter 5:8)

Under God, endings are unto beginnings; godly
sorrow unto redemption. Until now Mordecai
has been acting in a quiet and hidden way.
Except for his regular enquiries about Esther's
welfare, and his report to her concerning the
king's life, there has been nothing particularly
noticeable about him. As for the disagreement
between him and the king's servants over his
refusal to bow down to Haman, as far as he
knew, that had been strictly between themselves.

Suddenly, Mordecai is transformed. From
being quiet and inconspicuous he is both seen
and heard, and in an unmistakable fashion. His
face is drawn and distorted; his sackcloth and
ashes proclaim his deep distress; his cry of
anguish rises clear for all to hear. Could this be
exhibitionism? That would be completely out of
character with the Mordecai we have come to

know. In view of the unselfishness already seen as part of his nature, it would certainly need more than a personal grievance to destroy his usual serenity. Already he had borne the scoldings and taunts of the king's servants, with no record of any noisy protestations on his part.

There was something much larger which had pierced his soul: the thrust of a diabolical weapon, no less. A whole people, his people, were to be annihilated. That thrust breached the protective wall of the dam surrounding his soul, and his anguish poured out in a flood, drowning all thoughts of self, public opinion, or immediate consequences. In brief, Mordecai was completely identified with his people in their need of deliverance. Do we know even a little of such identification with the needs of God's people?

"I and my father's house have sinned," cried Nehemiah (Nehemiah 1:6) on hearing of the ruined state of the walls of Jerusalem, even though the disaster was far removed from his comfortable position in the king's palace. It might be said that such public manifestations of grief such as Mordecai and Nehemiah displayed belong to other times and customs. True, but the basic principle remains the same. We are *"workers together with Him"* (2 Corinthians 6:1).

In answer to His disciples' question, *"Why could we not cast it out?"* (Mark 9:29), after He had cast out the unclean spirit from the boy, Jesus told them, *"This kind cannot be driven out by anything but prayer."* Some ancient authorities add, *"and fasting"*. This kind of intercession unto redemption means a total identification of ourselves with those in need, as well as sacrificial prayer from the heart.

Not only was Mordecai identified with his people in their need of deliverance, but also he was himself being initiated into a work of deliverance, through this baptism of grief, confession and deepest intercession. There is no better introduction to active service for God than the humbling experience of confession and supplication. He was to be a link between despair and deliverance; and God needed a broken and contrite spirit through which to work.

Why did Mordecai refuse the garments Esther had so thoughtfully sent him, in order that he might cast off his sackcloth? It was not the time for such a change. He had not yet prayed through to the answer to the problem. Until then he must continue to intercede for deliverance. All this was a much needed preparation for the victory to come.

Is this the reason we do not see more deliverances? We fail to pray through, to go on bearing one another's burdens in continuing intercession, until God shows the way out.

Mordecai must have known that his refusal to accept the garments Esther had sent to replace his sackcloth and ashes could only serve to demonstrate the depth of his grief. He knew that Esther would make enquiries, and that this may well open up the way to acquainting her with the terrible news. Even though the gulf separating them, because of Esther's exalted position, was only a superficial one, it could well intensify danger. How longingly he must have awaited her next move.

There was not long to wait. Upon receiving back the garments, Esther had immediately sent Hathach to find out from Mordecai just what had happened. When the two men met outside the king's gate, Mordecai gave Hathach exact details of the events, and handed him a copy of the decree issued for the destruction of the Jews for him to give to Esther. Then followed these significant words, *"Charge her to go to the king to make supplication to him and entreat him for her people."*

It was a difficult order, but not one he himself would have shirked had he been in her position. Was he not committing himself totally to the ministry of intercession with the King of kings? If we ourselves have experienced something of what we ask others to do, spiritual weight is given to our words.

Even tragedy itself can present some ridiculous aspects to the ill-informed. Imagine the man in the street sending orders to the queen! Sackcloth and ashes would not be allowed inside the king's gate, never mind the palace court. Yet this humble man of God was in a strong position. Scorning mere appearances, he was set on obeying God and saving His people from destruction.

But there was the anguish and terrible isolation of his position. Esther must have seemed a long way off. Would the bond between them hold across the gap dividing them? It was no easy command he had sent her. It was coming from desperate need into the heart of luxury; from hopeless grief into the lightheartedness of court; from the threat of terrible disaster into the easy security of high position. Would the command penetrate Esther's heart? Would she feel the anguish behind the command? Above all, would she obey him just as when she was brought up by him?

As he paced up and down outside the king's gate, he pondered on Esther's sterling qualities. Who better than he to know them? Yet tragedy has a way of straining even the deepest relationships as fears bow down upon the soul. What a strength it is when God-given relationships hold fast in the day of testing. If God is in control, and it His will, the bond of unity will hold. Such an association is always unto something higher than those immediately concerned; something in the nature of redemption, of extending God's kingdom, of bringing glory to His Name.

It is not difficult to imagine Esther's distress when she received Mordecai's message and the copy of the decree. Even though she would share his grief over the threat to their people, his charge that she should go to the king to plead their cause must have filled her with acute alarm. It was not simply a matter of causing royal displeasure, but also a question of the law. She could only break this at her immediate peril.

41

Esther's answer to Mordecai was to make this crystal clear, *"All the king's servants and the people of the king's provinces know that if any man or woman goes to the king inside the inner court without being called, there is but one law; all alike are to be put to death, except the one to whom the king holds out the golden sceptre that he may live. And I have not been called to come in to the king these thirty days."*

Mordecai was one of the *"people of the king's provinces"* and already knew this. If Esther obeyed him she would be breaking the law. But in refusing to do obeisance to Haman had not Mordecai broken an equally important law, forfeiting his own life? The point about this dedicated man was that he not only put God right above such things as appearances and public opinion, but also above the law itself.

This threat to God's people was evil through and through, and no law was going to stand in the way of that evil being wiped out. God was not on the side of evil but of good, and he, Mordecai, was remaining firmly on the side of good. The humble Mordecai, of the hidden ministry, was suddenly revealed as being a mighty man of God. How good it is to await God's time. How much we miss and forfeit by not doing so. Insufficient discipline and preparation may mean that we are unable to meet the major challenge when it comes.

Mordecai loved Esther, and he must have realised what this sudden fearful test would cost her. His rearing of her had proved he was tender and unselfish. But he was faithful to God first, and then faithful to her. The substance of his message was a warning to her. Up until then he had instructed her not to reveal her kindred or her people. Now that these people were being seriously threatened, it would be morally wrong for her to hide this fact any longer.

The faithful Mordecai made it clear that if Esther refused to intervene on their behalf, then the intervention would come from another quarter. In other words, if there was no acceptance of the challenge, there would be no repeat of the challenge; and, for her at least, no victory out of the challenge.

Opportunities can come again, but the situation is never quite the same. Saddest of all is the victory that is never allowed to come about; the victory that would have been ours, under God, if we had accepted the challenge.

This was God's call to Esther, a call for her to do what no one else could do. It was now or never.

Mordecai's warning to Esther was one of the most solemn it is possible to make. Would she accept the personal peril involved in meeting the challenge? The fate of a whole people hung in the balance. It was like the awesome hush on the eve of battle, or the ominous silence before the storm.

"And who knows whether you have not come to the kingdom for such a time as this?"

With these words light suddenly broke through the pitch black clouds, gilding the harsh outlines of that challenge. Could this indeed be her hour of destiny, something far greater than herself or her personal life? All that had gone before had led up to this moment; all the careful upbringing, the gradual introduction to court life, the continuing, unquestioning obedience to Mordecai as God's representative; all had converged on this supreme moment in her life.

"For such a time as this . . . for such a time as this". Could she resist so clear, so divine a call? Never! Her whole being rose to meet the challenge. Her answer to Mordecai was beginning to take shape in her thoughts.

We never know when God's hour of destiny may strike. The need to be prepared for what God is purposing goes on throughout our Christian experience. If we allow ourselves to be prepared, our whole lives will become a steady fulfilment of God's plan for us.

Esther's answer to Mordecai shows her assessment, as well as her acceptance, of the challenge. Her assessment of its urgency and importance is revealed in her call for immediate prayer and fasting, to which she and her maids would also pledge themselves. There was to be no rushing into action, but rather a calm deliberation resulting from quiet waiting upon God. The waiting and fasting were to last not an hour or so, but three days and nights.

Perhaps if we were to know a small fraction of such an experience, it would take a great deal of the stress and strain out of life. It might even mean greater victories.

Esther's victory was complete. Nothing was left out. After fasting she would go to the king. The depth of her acceptance of the challenge can be measured by the six short, almost casual words, *"and if I perish, I perish."* She had become a participant in God's plan of deliverance for His people. More than this, the whole responsibility of changing the king's attitude towards their plight rested upon her alone.

Mordecai went away and *"did everything as Esther had ordered him"*. How gladly he would do so. Was it not for this that he had prayed, worked and waited?

Esther, composed and refreshed after her fast, put on her royal apparel. Then, clothed from head to foot in regal magnificence, she proceeded to the inner court where she stood alone, poised and ready. Even that splendid courage would have availed nothing had she entered the king's presence unsuitably attired.

Whether brave or cowardly, strong or weak, believing or fearful, as sinners, we have but one covering acceptable to the King of kings:

Jesus, Thy blood and righteousness
My beauty are, my glorious dress;
'Midst flaming worlds, in these arrayed,
With joy shall I lift up my head.[1]

1. Zinzendorf, tr. J. Wesley

Esther's glittering world might well have gone up in flames. But she stood there alone, steadfast, in that place of mortal danger.

Oh that it might be said of us that we are there at the heart of the need, not on the fringe of it, not where expediency permits, but where the laid-down life can bear fruit! There is an inner court in the soul of every man, much more hidden, much less dramatic, that the one mentioned here; but there to be entered into or ignored. The challenge to the Christians is, am I *"given up to death for Jesus' sake"* (2 Corinthians 4:11)? How much easier it is to by-pass this inner court, to avoid the issue, and thus to miss the glory as well as the cross.

Esther did not die.

"What is it Queen Esther?" The question was gentle and solicitous.

The king's first reaction to Esther, when he suddenly noticed her standing in the forbidden place, was one of favour. God was overruling his thoughts and feelings. There was no doubt about his eagerness in wanting to help her, even to the half of his kingdom.

"What is your request? It shall be given you, even to the half of my kingdom."

No panic, no hesitation marred the crucial moment when Esther made her request to the king, *"If it pleases the king, let the king and Haman come this day to a dinner that I have prepared for the king."*

But what about the all-important request concerning God's people? Were they not in imminent peril? And was not this a unique opportunity which might never be repeated? Yet there was no word about the matter, not one word. What kind of time was this for a banquet?

How often we spoil an opening into a person's life by being too much in a hurry. There are times when we have to act quickly, but these are rare. Esther had to feel her way, tracing God's path through an utterly pagan and alien atmosphere. This can be very slow and difficult work. In music the touch of the artist can be the most revealing feature of a finished performance. The touch is the expression of what lies behind it, and will reveal the quality of the performer. What better parable is there of our spiritual touch on other lives?

Esther began her urgent task, not by asking, but by giving. She invited these two enemies of her people to a meal, not only to do her best for them, but also that a right atmosphere might be created in which to make her difficult request. This story is set on a lavish oriental scale, but there is a lesson for us in our approach to people. Esther had all the servants she could want to help her, but she alone could gauge the quality of things, and the measure in which they would please her guests.

All this giving was geared to Esther's unswerving purpose, the saving of her people. Never for a moment did she forget their plight; there must have been considerable strain in watching the would-be murderers gorging themselves on the food she had provided. But

Esther knew how to wait. She had an outstanding example in Mordecai.

What God manifested of His wisdom and His power through Esther lives on for all time in this record. Nothing gives God a greater opportunity to act than a wholly dedicated man or woman. All God requires of us is a life offered willingly through which to work out His will and purposes.

Chapter 5

Everything
Going his Way

(Esther Chapter 5:9 - Chapter 6:9)

Once again the light is focused on Haman. This time it is with that special brilliance which so often precedes the darkness. Haman was riding high. Everything appeared to be going his way. Esther had let no one but him come to the banquet with the king, and there was the promise of a further banquet to which he and the king had been exclusively invited. Could anything be more promising?

There was one fly in the ointment: the Jew, Mordecai. Haman had passed him at the king's gate on his way out. It still rankled to see Mordecai sitting there, unmoving, when everyone else was bowing and doing him obeisance. How vulnerable is pride on its false foundation.

Haman restrained himself and hurried home to tell his wife and friends of his great good fortune. They, on their part, must have sat spell-bound as he spoke to them of the splendour of his riches, the number of his sons, the pre-eminence of his position above all the king's princes and servants, and, of course, the supreme honour of being invited a second time with the king to the queen's banquet. Why, his audience must have been transported with him up to the very heights of exultation!

Even at this moment of personal triumph among those closest to him, the inner poison had to come out. *"Yet all this does me no good,"* he told them bitterly, *"so long as I see Mordecai, the Jew, sitting at the king's gate."* Mordecai's doom was sealed by royal decree, yet Haman knew no peace, so fiercely burned the fire of hatred within him. It was this fire that ignited the feelings of his wife, Zeresh, giving incentive to a further plot, which was to spell out all too clearly Haman's own destruction.

God was nowhere within the distorted vision of Haman. Much too pressing were his immediate preoccupations. A gallows fifty cubits high was to be made right away and with all speed. *"Their feet run to evil, and they make haste to shed blood"* (Proverbs 1:16) was the very nature of that enterprise. The gallows had to be ready before the next morning, when Haman without delay would tell the king to have Mordecai hanged upon it.

Why the feverish haste? Up until then

everything had been deliberate and well thought out. Could it be that at the heart of this evil man there was a growing fear of the moral stature of that one man sitting at the king's gate? Was that why he had to be got rid of right away? This we do know. Haman never went *"merrily with the king to the dinner"*, because Mordecai was never hanged on the gallows.

That very same night on which Haman and his helpers were so feverishly building the gallows, the king too was awake. A deep compulsion drove him to ask for the Book of Chronicles to be brought to him. Why should it have happened on that particular night, when evil men were plotting evil deeds, that the king should have been pondering the valiant deeds of valiant men? Why should the king's attention have been drawn to Mordecai's saving act on his behalf, just when Mordecai's own life was being threatened? Coincidence? There are no coincidences in God's perfect timing.

Night or very early morning, under cover of darkness, can be the very incubator of evil deeds. It can, on the other hand, through its very stillness, be the time of deepest spiritual revelation. To the king, out of the blue, comes a most timely reminder of a good man, who, unknown to him, is in mortal danger. The best of memories can at times be unreliable. But God is always reliable, and therefore always on time. It was not in the divine plan that Mordecai should die.

As he pondered again Mordecai's earlier and

most loyal action, the king's heart was filled with gratitude. But there was also some misgiving. *"What honour or dignity has been bestowed on Mordecai for this?"* he asked his servants.

"Nothing has been done for him," came the reply.

As the king feared, the debt had never been paid.

Has our debt ever been paid? We owe a debt infinitely greater that that which the king owed Mordecai. Through Christ's death and resurrection, not only have we been saved from hell and destruction, but also we have obtained eternal life and blessedness.

Ingratitude is not only unjust, it can be dangerous. Had the king taken to heart and acknowledged what Mordecai had done when it was first reported to him, the plot against God's people might never have materialised. Mordecai would have been the one to be honoured, not Haman.

It is when we neglect to give God all we have and are, as a token of our profound gratitude for what He has done for us, that the devil can get a foothold in our lives. The safest and the most fruitful life is the all-out life. There will be no room for the enemy. It is thus that some small fraction of the debt we owe God can be paid.

Just at the moment of the king's discovery of the unpaid debt to Mordecai, Haman entered the court of the palace, eager to speak with the king about having Mordecai hanged on the gallows that he had prepared for him.

"*Let him come in,*" ordered the king.

Thus the king, his heart full of love, confronts a man whose heart is full of hate. Therefore, hate, the apparent master in the hour of Haman's seeming triumph, becomes, in effect, the very slave of love.

Haman, face to face with the king after a night of intense preparation for the annihilation of the man he most hated, was at the peak of his ambition. Not even his brilliant success in having gained royal assent to the plan for the destruction of the Jews had satisfied him. No, there was still that one fly in the ointment. There was still Mordecai, the man who had refused to bow down to him as the head of all things under the king, the man whose moral fibre presented a serious threat to his advancement.

Everything was ready for Mordecai's destruction. The gallows were complete. Only the king's consent remained to be secured. His royal master seemed to be in a very expansive mood. What was that he was saying? "*What shall be done to the man whom the king delights to honour?*" Why, the king is all out to please me! I must make the best I can of this. Who indeed would the king delight to honour more than me? The Mordecai matter must wait.

Haman's voice was smooth and engaging, "*Let royal robes be brought, which the king has worn, and the horse which the king has ridden, and on whose head a royal crown is set,"* (the voice became even smoother) *"and let the robes and the horse be handed over to one of the king's most noble princes; let him array the man whom the king delights to honour,"* (surely he had now reached the crest of his vision!) *"and let him conduct the man on horseback through the open square of the city,"* (could he not hear those cheers going up?) *"proclaiming before him: 'Thus shall it be done to the man whom the king delights to honour'."* Had ever a man achieved so personal a triumph?

Chapter 6

The Tables are Turned

(Esther Chapter 6:10-14)

At the very apex of Haman's exaltation an ice-cold hand clutched at his heart. What is this the king is now saying to him, "Make haste, take the robes and the horse, as you have said, and do so to Mordecai, the Jew who sits at the king's gate. Leave out nothing, Haman, nothing that you yourself have mentioned." Oh the supreme irony of it! His own words were falling back on his own head like sharp, piercing hail stones. Can anything be as blind, as isolating and self-destroying as pride?

We can imagine Haman, full of inner turmoil and torment, arriving at the king's gate, where the quiet, unobtrusive Mordecai was sitting, and hustling him out of his seat with some spluttered command, as from the king, and into a back room of the palace. There one of the king's eunuchs would rush in with the royal garments, and Haman would proceed to array his hated foe (no mention of one of the "most noble princes" doing it!) in the apparel which he had so coveted.

After this we see him conducting Mordecai on horseback through the open square of the city, proclaiming, *"Thus shall it be done to the man whom the king delights to honour."* Every moment of these proceedings would have been a veritable agony of frustration and disappointment for Haman.

For Mordecai, so wholly unprepared for such a startling development, it must have meant ceaseless and growing amazement. How was he to know that the king had suddenly remembered his report of the threat to his royal person? It is likely that Mordecai had forgotten the incident, preoccupied as he was with the plight of his people. He could not know that his action in saving the king's life was the key that opened the door to the deliverance so longed for.

To be thrust suddenly into the dazzling light of publicity and acclaimed as one whom the king honoured was the last thing he desired. For Esther, yes! For God's people, yes! Let them be saved, freed, honoured. Sackcloth and ashes, such as he had worn at the king's gate, were good enough for him. Somehow we cannot help feeling that he was glad to get back to that customary and inconspicuous place.

This is the person God delights to honour. Oh that such a selfless flame might burn within our hearts for the salvation of others.

Haman, in his moment of anguish, fled to his house, *"mourning and with his head covered"*, but there was no help there; only the stark truth, as spelt out by his wife and closest friends. We are not even told that they sought to comfort him. He had never lacked company. Not for him that kind of moral courage that can stand alone, awaiting the vindication of a righteous cause. Like a sand castle in the midst of a rising tide, his inner life was collapsing.

Feverish activity, like a drug, may hide the corruption and, even more tragically, the deep spiritual poverty of the inner life. But sooner or later, sometimes quite suddenly, we are made aware of that vast inner desert, and then who can help us?

It is at such a time that a man clutches at friends. Haman's friends could not help him, but at least they did not try to deceive him. For if his own vision was darkened by overwhelming fears, theirs suffered no such impediment. *"If Mordecai, before whom you have begun to fall, is of the Jewish people,"* they told him, *"you will not prevail against him but will surely fall before him."*

Why were they so sure? All down the centuries, wherever there have been Jews, men of other races and religions have felt their basic strength, their extraordinary independence, and the impact of their outstanding gifts. Something of this knowledge must have influenced these friends of the doomed man. Could this same knowledge, even if unconscious, have been the cause of Haman's hatred of Mordecai?

Even as his wife and friends were talking with him, he was being unceremoniously hurried out of his house, and taken to the queen's banquet. Had not this second invitation to a private and exclusive feast for the king, the queen and himself seemed the very apex of royal approval? Now, it could but emphasise his desperate position. What sort of tragic farce would be played out to the end?

Chapter 7

A Time to Speak Up

(Esther Chapter 7:1 – Chapter 8:3)

Esther stands out impressively against this dark background of human degradation. Far from showing any haste or panic, the crisis brought into relief her inimitable spirit. We have seen what lay behind it: her unfailing obedience to Mordecai; her calm acceptance of the risk to her life on entering the inner court of the palace uninvited; her continued patience in the midst of an abiding threat to herself and her people. In brief, she was an instrument tempered and conditioned for just such a test as now faced her.

The first feast had taken place, yet no word had Esther spoken of the great burden on her heart. She had no doubt decided that at the second banquet the king would be even more relaxed and approachable than at the first. Indeed, it was there that he again asked her,

"What is your petition, Queen Esther? It shall be granted you. And what is your request? Even to the half of my kingdom, it shall be fulfilled."

The first thing we notice about Esther's reply is that it is pervaded by a spirit of deep humility and respect for the king, *"if I have found favour in your sight, O king, and if it please the king."* There is nothing ingratiating about it. The agonising sense of the wrong to be inflicted upon her people was brought into complete subjection to the ruler of those people. How like the individual feelings and expressions of each musician in an orchestra, which must be brought under the complete control of the conductor.

Esther's request was put simply and succinctly, *"Let my life be given me at my petition, and my people at my request. For we are sold, I and my people, to be destroyed, to be slain, and to be annihilated. If we had been sold merely as slaves, men and women, I would have held my peace; for our affliction is not to be compared with the loss to the king."* She placed her request within the bounds of a superior authority. Its effectiveness was dependent upon that authority.

Only within the bounds of the divine will can our petitions have any effectiveness or value. They must begin and end with the King of kings.

At the end of her request, Esther sought to get away from her own and her people's position to the king's. She was saying, in effect, that, if they were to be sold as slaves, the king would gain from this, and she would have no case to plead; their sufferings in slavery could not be compared with the king's greater loss of so much man-power. But the king had nothing to gain from their annihilation.

She was a woman well-schooled in the grace of submission, and a very wise woman. This "Mother in Israel" was holding her life-and-death petition, literally the only hope of thousands, well within the compass of the king's will and prerogative.

As the presence of poison in the body must be exactly located before it can be dispelled, so must evil in the soul be clearly identified before it can be properly dealt with.

"Who is he, and where is he, that would presume to do this?" asked the king, seeking for the one responsible for the threat described by Esther.

This, at last, was her long-awaited moment. She was wholly ready for it. Her eyes must have flashed as she singled out the man who, once powerful, now cringed before her. *"A foe and enemy! This wicked Haman!"*

Not only was Haman's guilt identified by attestation, but it was also intensified by appearances. As the king *"in wrath"* went out into the palace garden, Haman, in terror for his life, and in a desperate attempt to appeal to Esther, lost control of himself and fell upon her couch. Upon re-entry, the king found him as if in the act of assaulting the queen, and his guilt appeared all the greater.

Suspicion, once roused, needs little encouragement to grow. Events began to move rapidly to their climax. God used three people to bring it about: Esther, Haman, and one of the king's eunuchs, who said to the king, *"Moreover, the gallows which Haman has prepared for Mordecai, whose word saved the king, is standing in Haman's house, fifty cubits high."*

And the king said, *"Hang him on that."*

Not only was Haman's guilt identified by attestation, and intensified through appearances, but also he was actually impaled to his own act. He was hanged on the very gallows on which he had planned to hang Mordecai. It is a sombre picture. In what it conveys, it is as final as the words, *"the wages of sin is death"* (Romans 6:23).

Like a streak of light breaking through the darkest clouds are the words of Paul, *"And you, who were dead in trespasses . . . God made alive . . . having cancelled the bond which stood against us with its legal demands; this He set aside, nailing it to the cross"* (Colossians 2:13-14). Christ Himself was impaled, not to His own act, but to the most terrible one ever perpetrated by humanity. In allowing this, and by voluntarily giving His life, He nailed our sin to that very cross on which He died.

From the recent tautness of anger the king now relaxed in an atmosphere of warmth and liberality. It was a day when both Esther and Mordecai received generous rewards from their grateful sovereign.

There never would have been a day when the king gave so lavishly if there had not been that night when he remembered his debt. It was because he had faced up to this failure, and had done all he could to put it right, that "on that day" the king took off his signet ring and gave it to Mordecai, and gave Esther a house.

This is always God's order. The wrong must be faced, must be put right, and the blessings will follow, as day follows night. And what blessings! There was no lingering blight on the spirit, no strained relationships, no unrelieved sense of guilt.

Esther had never asked for a house. She had petitioned the king more than once, on behalf of her people, because of their mortal danger. A house was nothing by comparison. Her whole life had been one of dedication. She had submitted herself to Mordecai's wise counsels in the early days; and this training had resulted in the thwarting of Haman's plot, and the saving of her people.

As Christians, serving the best of all masters, do we know any thing of this spirit of self-sacrifice? How different is such a life from one given over to the pursuit of happiness, or to the obtaining and keeping of our rights. But are not these things natural and legitimate? Certainly they are. Yet the words of our Lord remain unchanged, "*It is more blessed to give than to receive*" (Acts 20:35); and the challenge in John's first epistle, "*By this we know love, that He laid down His life for us; and we ought to lay down our lives for the brethren*" (1 John 3:16), is still ours today.

Surprises such as Esther was experiencing were all the sweeter for being unexpected. A house of her own! This would not be a palace where she must always act as queen, but a private residence where she could be herself. Even if she had not anticipated a personal token coming from the king to her, she was well aware that some royal gift might be bestowed on the man to whom she owed so much. *"And Mordecai came before the king,"* we read, *"for Esther had told what he was to her"*. The king placed the very ring that he had taken away from Haman on the hand of Mordecai.

The house of Haman, the home of that evil man, was now to be hers. If she had any misgivings on account of its previous owner, she put them behind her as she gave her most trusted friend full control of it, *"she set Mordecai over the house of Haman"*.

God delights to give to His people that which has been usurped by His enemies, *"Every place that the sole of your foot will tread upon* (enemy territory) *have I given to you"* (Joshua 1:3). No spiritual triumph is greater than to prove God's victory in the very place once owned by Satan.

Haman, the hater of the Jews, was dead. Mordecai, their defender, occupied the place of power, once held by this evil foe. But the threat to the Jews still remained, because Haman's edict against them had not been revoked. The poison had been identified, drawn and dispelled, but the effects of that poison remained in the body.

There was a change in Esther's approach to the king. Previously, she had spoken calmly and with dignity, even with great power, as on the last occasion. Now her control has been swept away by the flood of her love and anguish for her people. She is defenceless in her grief.

In our prayers for others, sometimes we can move on quickly to the identifying and stating of the need, and from there to intercession. At other times, however, the process is much slower.

King Ahasuerus was a pagan despot. Esther had known instinctively that it would not be wise to show too much feeling at first. It was what she was, or appeared to be, that would make or mar her chances of having her request granted.

Because Jesus is our great high priest, we can approach the King of kings, the Lord God Himself. *"Let us then with confidence draw near to the throne of grace, that we may receive mercy and find grace to help in time of need"* (Hebrews 4:16). Times and customs may be vastly different from what they were for Esther, but certain basic essentials, such as honesty, tact and patience remain the same in all ages.

Love is the key-note. All along, love has prompted this dedicated woman's actions. Now love overflows into tears. *"She fell at his feet and besought him with tears to avert the evil designs of Haman the Agagite and the plot which he had devised against the Jews"*. This was the very limit of her appeal to the king. In abasing herself she could go no lower. In her impassioned plea, she could go no further.

Do we, as Christians, go as far as this in our intercession with God? There is a spiritual, if not physical, prostration of ourselves before the Lord, an actual giving of spirit, soul and body in our supplication for the souls of men. Paul reminds us that *"we are not contending against flesh and blood, but against the principalities, against the powers, against the world rulers of this present darkness, against the spiritual hosts of wickedness in the heavenly places"* (Ephesians 6:12), and that *"though we live in the world we are not carrying on a worldly war, for the weapons of our warfare are not worldly but have divine power to destroy strongholds"* (2 Corinthians 10:3,4).

God's word to Israel was, *"If my people who are called by my name humble themselves, and pray and seek my face, and turn from their wicked ways, then I will hear from heaven, and will forgive their sin and heal their land"* (2 Chronicles 7:14).

The believer's direct approach to God Himself has a deeper significance than Esther's approach to the king, but the complete and humble self-giving in intercession is the same.

Chapter 8

An Extended Sceptre

(Esther Chapter 8:4-8)

As Esther lay prostrate at the king's feet, forgetful of all but her passionate intercession for her people, something happened. The king did not speak, for no word is recorded. But some instinct, some premonition, must have made her look up just as the gilded sceptre was being held out to her. The shining of that symbol of royal authority must have been as a shaft of light piercing the darkness of her soul.

All was not lost. A new hope lifted her spirit as she rose to her feet in obedience to the king's implied command. What was his wish? Had she not already besought him when lying at his feet? Now he obviously awaited a calm and distinct statement of her petition.

We are reminded of the blind man who was told that Jesus was passing by (Mark 10:46-52). Our Lord was fully aware of this man's agony as he besought him to have mercy on his pitiable condition, but He did not immediately respond to his request. Instead, He commanded that he should be brought to Him.

"*What do you want me to do for you?*" asked Jesus.

"*Master,*" came the prompt reply, "*let me receive my sight.*"

Christ always responds when our need of Him is deep and sincere. But He likes our requests to be clear and definite.

"*You do not have, because you do not ask*" (James 4:2).

Solomon reminds us that there is "*a time for every matter under heaven*"; among other things, "*a time to break down, and a time to build up*" (Ecclesiastes 3:3). Any remaining barrier of resistance in the king would surely have been finally melted by Esther's tears. The breakdown had occurred; now was the time to build. We do not build while lying down. Esther rose to her feet and stood. The last position in affirming our faith in God, and in facing the enemy, is that of standing. "*Having done all . . . stand,*" says Paul (Ephesians 6:13).

We see Esther, all her emotions under complete control, standing calm and utterly deferential to the one whose authority was superior to her own. She approached the king, with her customary form of address, and clearly and boldly stated her request to "*let an order be written to revoke the letters devised by Haman . . . which he wrote to destroy the Jews who are in all the provinces of the king."*

So wise had been this dedicated woman's conduct in all her approaches to the king, that not once had he refused her requests. This final and all-important request was to be no exception. It cannot be over-stressed that conduct, consistent with that which is right, thoughtful of others, and careful in every detail, is of the utmost importance. The ground for Esther's success had been well and truly laid.

Two people, the king and Haman, had forged the plot to destroy the Jews; two people, Esther and Mordecai, had worked to defeat that plot. Now three people, the king, Esther and Mordecai, were working as one to bring about the great deliverance.

Not long before these three were widely separated: one on his throne, at the height of power; one sitting at the king's gate, with seemingly no power at all; and the other, as queen, the essential link between the two. As they move towards the supreme purpose of their lives, they are drawn ever closer together until they are acting as one, single, indivisible unit.

Three is a strong number, referred to many times in the Scriptures as such. *"There are three witnesses, the Spirit, the water, and the blood; and these three agree"* (1 John 5:7). On the highest level of all, there is the Trinity: God, the Father, God, the Son, and God, the Holy Spirit.

A tripod of strength headed the nation. Our Lord said, *"To him who has will more be given, and he will have abundance; but from him who has not, even what he has will be taken away"* (Matthew 13:12). It is a truth graphically portrayed here. Haman lost even the seeming power he had. Mordecai had always had the queen's support; now was added the all-powerful authority of the king. It was a three-fold cord, not to be broken.

What is note-worthy is the intrinsic difference between the ground on which the king approved of Haman's plot for the destruction of the Jews, and the ground on which he supported Esther's plan for their deliverance. The first was an appeal to the king's pride, "(the Jews) *do not keep the king's laws, so that it is not for the king's profit to tolerate them,*" and was sustained by a bribe, "*I will pay ten thousand talents of silver . . . into the king's treasuries*" (ch.3:8-9). The second, Esther's ground, had nothing to do with the king's pride, or personal prestige. It was simply love.

Esther's tears, while prostrate at the king's feet, may have melted any remaining resistance within him, but her words, bravely spoken, as she stood face to face with him, must have affected him even more deeply, "*For how can I endure to see the calamity that is coming to my people? Or how can I endure to see the destruction of my kindred?*"

No need for a bribe here. Love can stand on its own merit. It is the greatest force in all the world. The king had seen a living expression of it in this woman's passionate and selfless dedication to the good of her people. There was no hesitation in his reply. Esther and Mordecai could write as they pleased with regard to the Jews, in the king's name, and seal it with the king's ring, *"for an edict written in the name of the king and sealed with the king's ring cannot be revoked."*

A Day of Violence

(Esther Chapter 8:9 - Chapter 9:15)

The slow and delicate period of preparation had succeeded. The great turning point was close at hand. The king's secretaries were summoned. The edict that Mordecai commanded to be written was to be sent from India to Ethiopia, to one hundred and twenty-seven provinces, in the script and language of each one, including that of the Jews.

It was in the first month, the month of Nisan, that Haman had issued his decree, with its special day of destruction, the thirteenth day of the twelfth month. Mordecai's decree was over two months later. Speed was of the essence. The letters were sent by *"mounted couriers riding on swift horses that were used in the king's service, bred from the royal stud"*.

Mordecai did not forbid the enemy forces from gathering on that fixed date. He could have done so, and prevented the terrible slaughter that was to take place. It is of deep significance that he did not do so. Judgment must always fall on sin.

Jesus confirmed the divine law of the Old Testament, and added to it, "*You have heard that it was said to the men of old, 'You shall not kill; and whoever kills shall be liable to judgment.' But I say to you that everyone who is angry with his brother shall be liable to judgment*" (Matthew 5:21).

Christ bore the divine judgment for our sins on the cross. Even in this day of grace, if we fail to appropriate His atonement for ourselves, we must come under condemnation, and be judged. This is inevitable because God is holy, and He cannot look upon sin.

There is another consideration here. The avoiding of a direct confrontation with the enemy would have denied God the visible triumph over that very enemy, and the demonstration before the nations of His greater glory.

The same idea is relevant in the spiritual realm. Paul's injunctions to Timothy to "*fight the good fight of faith*" (1 Timothy 6:12), and to the Ephesians to "*put on the whole armour of God, that you may be able to stand against the wiles of the devil*" (Ephesians 6:11), bear out the inescapable fact that we are to face our mortal foe, and by God's strength and protection to prevail against him. There is no greater testimony to the power of God than that the world should see the result of such victories.

Certainly, there are occasions when God tells us to flee. Lot was warned to escape from Sodom on the eve of divine judgment (Genesis 19:15). Jesus tells us to *"flee from the wrath to come"* (Matthew 3:7). There are extreme situations (often brought on by our own sin and failure), when, in His mercy, God does *"make a way of escape"* (1 Corinthians 10:13). However, the normal position for the committed Christian is a resolute facing up to the challenge of contending for the faith.

The Jews knew from Mordecai's edict that the thirteenth day of the twelfth month was still the day of the battle with their enemies. They knew also that they would be taking the initiative, and that their opponents would be utterly destroyed.

It is not difficult to imagine the stature Mordecai gained in the eyes of his released people. When this benefactor left the presence of the king, clad in his royal robes, a golden crown upon his head, the whole city of Susa shouted for joy. Few men are worthy of such honour and deep feeling. The clever and the powerful can dazzle with their brilliance, or crush by their authority; but there is a depth of warmth and gratitude which belongs only to those who are dedicated to the good of others.

In the humblest Jewish home, there was *"light and gladness and joy and honour"*, and the battle had not yet been fought, nor the victory won. How could this be? We look for the explanation

74

in the fact that Mordecai's edict was written in the king's own name, and sealed with the king's own ring.

There is a higher authority than that of any earthly king. Joshua had that authority when God, as *"commander of the Lord's army"* (Joshua 5:14), appeared to him on the eve of the fall of Jericho. This divine visitor said to Joshua, *"See, I have given into your hand Jericho, with its king and mighty men of valour"* (Joshua 6:2).

We can go still deeper into this matter by remembering Christ's own words in John, Chapter sixteen, verse thirty-three, *"In the world you will have tribulation"* (the battle will occur, and must be faced), *"but be of good cheer"* (now, before the battle), *"I have overcome the world"* (His victory, to be worked out through us, is already won!)

In our hearts, too, there can be *"light, gladness, joy and honour"*, as there was in those Jewish homes; not only after but also before the victory to be manifested. Then our light will *"shine before men"* (Matthew 5:16). They will not know whether we are facing, going through, or have finished the battle; but they will see the light.

"Let your light shine before men, that they may see your good works and give glory to your Father who is in heaven" (Matthew 5:16). It is the fact that they might "see" that matters so desperately.

Suddenly, from the light and gladness in Jewish homes, the situation is plunged into darkness, the darkness of violence, slaughter, and total destruction.

It is easy to be revolted by these horrific scenes. We tend to think they belong to the Old Testament, to another age. But are we, in our day, any further advanced when it comes to matters of cruelty? Such conflicts were noisy, callous, and brutal in the extreme; but at least men met face to face. They had some chance, however remote, of defending themselves. In the Second World War what chance of self-protection was there for the men, women and children who were herded into the gas chambers? Even their screams, their last remaining human expression, were silenced. Could any noise of battle compare to the awfulness of that silence?

Sin remains sin, whether in ancient or modern times. The Jews were sinners, just as were their opponents. But they had been the near-victims of a most ghastly plot, and therefore, in social terms, were more sinned against than sinning. The whole of this battle, then, was one of retribution. Even Esther's request that the ten slain sons of Haman should be hanged on the same gallows as those used for their father's death, should be viewed in this light. It was the old law of " *an eye for an eye and a tooth for a tooth*" (Exodus 21:24). Until Christ came and brought a new dimension in moral conduct, it was the law.

Yet, there was a deeper, wider, and higher reason than all this. It had to do with God's over-all purposes, and His greater glory. The Jews were His chosen people. If Haman had succeeded, it would not have been the safety of the Jews in Persia alone that would have been endangered, but, because Persia was the supreme power in Jerusalem and throughout Asia, the Jews everywhere would probably have perished.

Chapter 10

A Day of Victory

(Esther Chapter 9:16 - Chapter 10:3)

The name of God is nowhere mentioned in this book. Yet how plainly has His hand been seen all along, anticipating evil, defeating and over-ruling it, to the deliverance of His people.

We have a supreme example of God's over-ruling purposes, His greater glory, in our Lord's earthly life. Everything He did was of utmost importance: His confrontation with and victory over Satan in the wilderness; His confrontation with and victory over His critics; His confrontation with and victory over the agony of Gethsemane. Towering above all these was His confrontation with and victory over death on the cross.

If the fight we engage in is on His side, if the issue is for His glory, then we can have the assurance of victory, even before the event, whatever the event may be.

The Book of Esther ends on a triumphant note. The victory was complete. The battle has been one of retribution. There is one sentence that occurs no less than three times, *"but they laid no hands on the plunder"*. It is very significant. Retribution there was to be, but not greed. The judgment was to be exactly commensurate with the evil judged; no more, no less. There were to be no extended acts of vengeance, no excessive gains. How perfect are God's scales of justice.

The Jews were not to forget their wonderful escape from disaster. As with that greater deliverance, when God brought His people out of the land of Egypt, so they were ever to remember His omnipotent acts on their behalf. Every year, two days, to be known as Purim, were to be set apart to commemorate their God-given victory.

We have only to study Old Testament passages such as these to realise the importance God gives to 'remembering'. This reminds us of Jesus words on the occasion of the healing of the ten lepers. *"Were there not ten cleansed? Where are the nine?"* (Luke 17:17). How easy it is to call on God for help at a time of need; but to forget, when the help is given, to thank the Giver.

In this age of grace, it is the spontaneous, continuous praise and thanksgiving from the heart, that God seeks, *"always and for everything giving thanks in the name of our Lord Jesus Christ to God the Father"* (Ephesians 5:20).

The character of Esther, both as woman and queen, is most striking. Through her devotion, her obedience, and her outstanding courage, God wrought the wonderful deliverance of His people. Without Esther, this particular manifestation of divine power would not have taken place.

Yet Mordecai, that humble, unknown man sitting at the king's gate day after day, was to prove the greatest single influence in guiding the young queen towards her true destiny. It is significant that, in the last two chapters of this Book, much stress is given to Mordecai's greatness and eminent position, a fulfilment of Jesus' words that *"the last shall be first"* (Matthew 19:30).

God works through individuals to fulfil His great purposes. It is not a question of how many people or what sort of gifts; it is a matter of personal dedication and self-giving service.

"God chose what is foolish in the world to shame the wise, God chose what is weak in the world to shame the strong, God chose what is low and despised in the world, even things that are not, to bring to nothing things that are, so that no human being might boast in the presence of God."
(1 Corinthians 1:27-29).